Made in the USA
Monee, IL
21 August 2021

76142781R00070